ISBN 978-0-331-10977-1
PIBN 11015119

MR. EMERSON's

DISCOURSE

BEFORE THE

HUMANE SOCIETY.

A

D.I S C O U R S E,

DELIVERED IN THE

FIRST CHURCH, BOSTON,

ON THE

ANNIVERSARY·

OF THE

MASSACHUSETTS

HUMANE SOCIETY.

June 9, 1807.

By WILLIAM EMERSON, A.A.S. S.H.S.

Pastor of the First Church in Boston.

BOSTON:

PRINTED BY MUNROE & FRANCIS,

NO. 10, COURT-STEET.

. . . .

1807.

RESPIRATION.

EZEK. XXXVII. 5.

BEHOLD, I WILL CAUSE BREATH TO ENTER INTO YOU, AND YE
SHALL LIVE.

THE entrance of breath into a body is essential
to its life. We are told of animals, which can live without food, but not without air. Deprived of limbs, of the
heart, and even of the head,[1] some reptiles are said to be
able to perform almost all the functions of life ; yet, as
soon as you interrupt the communication between their
lungs and the atmosphere, they languish ; cut it off en-
tirely, and they die. The smallest insect refuses the gift
of life, if denied the privilege of respiration ; and the
fish itself expires in convulsions under the exhausted re-
ceiver.

, We grant indeed that nature is not forward to reveal
her secrets ; and we are grateful for that principle of ac-
commodation, by which she adapts her subjects to their
condition and circumstances. We have heard of animals

---

[1] See an account of the experiments of Spalanzani and others on frogs.
Encyclop. Brittan. art. Physiology.

enclosed in stones and in trees, of serpents and polypi congealed with the frost, and of the swallow and the dormouse in brumal retirement.[2] We have also been made somewhat acquainted with the conjectures of the curious on these wonderful stories. After all, we receive with caution the seeming exceptions to the general law, demanding air for the maintenance of life.

It is the power of respiration that distinguishes a living from a dead body, inert matter from its animated forms, glowing nature from the imitations of art. The beautiful portrait gives us pleasure, and the statue of exquisite workmanship commands our admiration, only in proportion to their resemblance of life ; and there is literally ' no good to the owners thereof, saving the beholding of them with their eyes.'[3] --When we approach them, we perceive the canvass to be breathless; and the marble cold. They are warmed by no spirit, and have no irritable fibres nor sensible nerves. Such was the

---

[2] The long disputed question, *whither do the swallows go in the winter?* seems not to have received a satisfactory solution : there are many hearsay stories concerning the matter, but no authenticated facts. - In *Morse's American gazetteer*, under art. scituate the following account promises somewhat towards answering the question.- " A Millpond in this town (Scituate) being suddenly drawn off by a breach in the dam, in the winter season, some years ago exhibited a matter of speculation to many of the inhabitants. The swine of the neighbourhood rooted up house swallows in great quantities from the spot which the water had left, which they ate greedily...Swallows have been found in several other places ; at Egg Harbour, in New-Jersey, in a marshy place, a large cedar being blown down, a vast number of swallows were found in the mud of the root." However, well informed the author of the American Gazetteer may have been with regard to the finding of swallows in the mud at " Egg Harbour and several other places," it is impossible for me to say , but on this point, as it respects Scituate, he was misinformed The Rev. Dr. Barnes of that place, a respectable philosopher as well as divine, has repeatedly assured me that, after a diligent inquiry into the story, he found it was without a tittle of truth.

[3] Eccles. v. 2.

body of our common progenitor, when the Lord God first 'formed him of the dust of the ground.'[4] . Eyes had he; but he saw not; ears, but he heard not; neither was there musick nor voice in the organs of speech, until his almighty maker 'breathed into his nostrils the breath of life.'. It was then that 'he became a living soul.'[4] His lungs, filled with air, commenced their regular operations. They retained a portion of what they received, transmitted it to appropriate cells, and, having used the remainder, returned it for a fresh supply of the uncontaminated atmosphere. The alternate expansion and contraction of the thorax maintained the process of respiration. The blood began its everlasting circulations through the pulmonary arteries. The lungs received it; exposed it to the action of the air; revivified its power; renewed its colour; and returned it to the heart, which poured it forth again into a thousand currents.

It was formerly believed that the lungs were moved, not, by any external agent, but by a certain expansile power, which themselves possessed. It is now ascertained that in man, and other warmblooded animals, respiration is performed by a diaphragm; and that in ordinary circulations the lungs are passive. Is the function of respiration then altogether involuntary? Without doubt involuntary for the most part; else man would have the power of breathing out his life at pleasure, and there would be no provision for sustaining it in seasons of sleep. It is affirmed, that one hundred and nine cubick inches of air will remain in his lungs, after his best efforts at complete expiration.[5] It is, however, happy for man,

---

[4] Gen. ii. 7.   [5] Bostock's Essay on Respiration, p. 35.

that his respiratory organs are in some measure subject to his will. Two hundred and eighty cubick inches, it seems, are contained in his lungs, when in their natural condition. He commonly employs no more than forty inches in a single act of respiration; yet is he capable of propelling from his lungs more than four times this quantity of air, after an ordinary expiration. Hence the power of speech, and all the infinite and pleasing variety of vocal musick.

That a principal benefit of respiration is the production of animal heat, is a supposition, which at this day, will hardly be controverted. But it first acts upon the air, and then upon the blood.

Respiration first acts upon the air. The atmosphere, in which we live, is not, as it should obviously seem to be, a simple element. It is composed of two distinct fluids, possessing different properties, and serving different purposes. One of them is friendly, the other destructive to animal life. To the great Dr. Priestley and the celebrated Lavoisier are the world indebted for the most valuable discoveries and beautiful experiments relating to this theory. These and other philosophers have proved to us that, of an hundred parts of atmospherick air, twenty-seven only consist of oxygen. This is the gas, which serves as food to the lungs, which gives to the lamp of life its lustre, and is essential to combustion in bodies universally. Seventy-two hundreths of the atmosphere are engrossed by azote, and one hundreth by carbonic acid. These gasses, when disengaged from oxygen, though fatal to the respiration of animals, have yet their important use. Pure oxygenous gas cannot long be inhaled with safety. Our creator has accordingly given us a modified atmosphere, in which to breathe, and thus defended our frame against a too rapid consumption.

Another instance of his infinite wisdom, in this connexion, is manifest in the contrariety of food, which is requisite for the support of animal and vegetable life. The oxygen, which to man and most other animals is the vital fluid, is rejected by plants as noxious to their existence, and issues from their bodies in a continual stream ; whilst the azotic gas, so poisonous to us, is inhaled by them with eagerness and delight.

In atmospheric air, thus compounded of two or rather three distinct principles, respiration produces a change. It diminishes the quantity of air by absorbing a portion of the oxygen gas ; it generates a quantity of fixed air in the lungs; it absorbs, probably, a very small quantity of azote[6] ; and it remits a portion of aqueous vapour. So that atmospheric air, which has been breathed, is found to contain a vastly larger portion of fixed air, a less portion of vital air, whilst the azotic air, unfit for the support of either life or flame, remains not sensibly, though, in a very small degree, lessened.

Respiration also acts upon the blood. The oxygenous part of the atmospheric air enters the vesciles of the lungs. The blood, possessing an attraction for oxygen, absorbs a portion of it, and immediately exchanges its purple for a vermillion colour. The oxygen, at first loosely united with the mass of blood, in the course of circulation, forms

---

[6] Lavoisier was not sensible of this ; but later experiments by Mr. Davy with more accurate instruments than his, determine, that a small portion of azote, viz. about $\frac{1}{160}$ part of the air respired, is absorbed.

B

a closer connexion with its carbon, whence an oxyd is produced. This oxydated blood loses its florid appearance ; it returns to the lungs ; it discharges a portion both of inflammable and of aqueous matter ; and is recreated and reddened by a new supply of oxygen. Respiration then frees the blood of two noxious principles, hydrogen and carbon ; and insinuates into it a new principle of vitality.

It is evident, that this process must be attended with the production of heat. Caloric, or the principle of heat, combines with different bodies in different degrees, and is the cause of fluidity in all. But it is a well known law of nature, that fluid, changing into solid bodies, or solid, changing into fluid bodies, extricate heat. The oxygen, taken into the blood, recedes from its gaseous state, and consequently heat is evolved. It is oxygen, which, by means of the blood, distributes itself through the parts of the body, and generates heat in all the extremities. This heat, evolved in some sensible form, preserves the irritability of the system. Yet the heat of an animal is not wholly derived from its lungs : the blood imbibes the matter of heat through the sensible warmth, which is externally applied to the body. The lungs are not so much the focus of animal heat, as the spark which enkindles it : they are not a kind of furnace, generating heat for the rest of the body, but, having imparted to the blood a vital principle, each part of the system is left, according to its degree of action, to generate heat for itself. The grand business of a living body is the constant assimilation of new parts. [7] To cause the new parts to pass

[7] Bell's Anat. Vol. 2. p. 125. Edin. edit. 1797.

from a fluid into a solid form is the object of all the circulations. The whole nourishment of the system proceeds in the extreme vessels, and is an uninterrupted assumption of new parts. The vessels are constantly occupied in forming acids, oxyds, and secretions. The consequence of this continual labour is a chemical change, and of this chemical change the consequence is continual heat.

Such are the intention, the offices, and the effects of respiration in living bodies. It is only when this power is unimpaired, that the animal can live in the enjoyment of health, vigour, and beauty.

In a contrast with this natural and happy condition, contemplate the effects of suspended respiration upon a human being. Suppose the mischief to have happened by an immersion in noxious air. The first efforts of the victim to inspire are instantly followed by a sensation in the trachea, that there is no provender of life in the fluid. He rejects the deleterious gas; and, the muscles of expiration continuing to act, the vital air is speedily expelled from the lungs, which as speedily collapse.

Similar are the effects of ordinary hanging. The power of expiration performs its office, whilst the trachea cannot be opened for the admission of air : of course the wretch is destroyed from a collapse of the lungs.

Nor are the consequences of drowning totally different. It is not from the intrusion of a little water into his lungs and stomach, that dissolution accrues to a drowning subject. On his first submersion, air is expired from the lungs; and he struggles in vain to supply the deficiency by inspiration. Air is again expelled; a small quantity more of water is received; but, in less than four minutes, the muscles of expiration cease to act, and convulsions are at an end.

Thus far we venture to affirm with some degree of confidence. But in our progress to investigate the proximate cause of apparent death, in the abovementioned cases, we are bewildered amidst the speculations of philosophers, and the facts of experimenters. Mr. Kite,[8] by a train of ingenious reasoning, not utterly destitute of support from observation, displays on this question a plausible theory. In his opinion, the consequence of suspended respiration is a congestion of blood in the right side of the heart and lungs. This congestion, he supposes, operates fatally, not on the heart nor on the lungs, but on the brain. Of course, his conclusion is, that those, who die by drowning, die of an apoplexy.

This theory, however specious, meets a powerful opposer in Dr. Edward Coleman. This physician alleges, that " in drowning and in suffocation from foul air, it has been found, that the veins of the head are not more distended than in natural death ; and that apoplexy does not take place, as has been supposed, from hanging, is equally true : for if such were the case, a recovery could not be effected ; since our endeavours to remove common apoplexy, even while the process of respiration and circulation proceed, frequently prove unsuccessful."[9]

By other arguments and a course of experiments, the last mentioned writer pretty satisfactorily establishes the doctrine, that apoplexy never happens in drowning, hanging, and suffocation ; that the immediate cause of the

---

[8] Essays and Observ. physiological and medical on the Submersion of Animals. Lond., 1795.

[9] A Dissertation on Natural and Suspended Respiration by E. Coleman. Second Edit. Lond. 1802. p. 261.

suspension of circulation is, " not the presence of black
blood in the left side of the heart, nor the mere want of
motion in the lungs, but a collapse of the air cells of the
lungs, which produces a mechanical obstruction to the
passage of the blood in the small branches of the pulmonary vessels."[10]

Here then the interesting question arises, By what
means shall the victims of casualty be rescued from
the jaws of death ? How shall the mechanical obstruction, which has followed a collapse of the lungs,
be removed ? What shall change the blood, and
stimulate the heart ? How shall the natural circulations be restored ? How, in a word, shall we CAUSE
BREATH TO ENTER INTO THESE BREATHLESS
FORMS, THAT THEY MAY LIVE ?

An answer to these queries is found in a variety of
treatises on this subject by medical and physiological
writers. We find, indeed, what might naturally be ex-
pected, slight variations with regard to the means, and
their use, of resuscitation ; yet the most respectable au-
thorities are, generally, agreed in the following reply.

Never by the smoke of tobacco, which uniformly in-
duces such a degree of debility in the human frame, as
the best powers of life are hardly able to support. Not
by bleeding, since the disease is not a compression of the
brain, except in instances where a previous disposition to
plethora prevailed, or external violence has been sustain-
ed. Nor yet by emetics, until the circulations are re-
established. A case of suspended respiration is that of
extreme debility, to which nothing surely should be added
to increase the evil. To pour poisons into the stomach

10 Coleman, p. 151.

of a man, breathless through submersion, is at once to quench that spark, which should be gently fanned into a flame : in direct repugnance to the example of him, who came, *not to destroy men's lives, but to save them*, it is violently ' breaking a bruised reed'.[11]

On the contrary, let the patient have the immediate benefit of gentle stimuli. Let the stomach be warmed with a generous cordial. Let the lungs be expanded, that they may feel the stimulus of the element they love ; but, in imitation of natural respiration, let them be alternately distended and collapsed. Electricity should also be directed to the heart, that every portion of its remaining irritability may be brought into action ; at the same moment, let the shock be uniformly attended with a concomitant expansion of the lungs. Let the access of cold air to the body be cautiously avoided ; and by the application of warmth prevent the escape of heat from the blood, and thus supply, as far as possible, the defect of that heat, which should have been absorbed from the air. When the lungs have been expanded and collapsed, the use of frictions may be advantageously commenced, and should be tenderly and diligently continued. " The final intention of the whole plan of treatment is," in the words of Dr. Coleman, " to imitate the natural circulation."[12] In every stage of the process let your moderation be known by slowly making haste.[13]

---

[11] Matt. xii. 20.　　　　　　　[12] Coleman, p. 272.

[13]　　　" While the vital fire
Burns feebly, heap not the green fuel on ;
But prudently foment the wandering spark,
With what the soonest feels its kindred touch ;
Be frugal even of that ; a little give
At first ; that kindled, add a little more,
Till, by deliberate nourishing, the flame,
Revived, with all its wonted vigour glows."　　　*Armst.*

It is in the use of these instruments of restoration, that the Royal Humane Society of London, and its offspring Institutions, under the blessing of almighty God, have redeemed thousands from a state, in which they soon would have slept the sleep of death.[14] It is by these means, my brethren and friends, members of the Humane Society, assembled in this place, that you are enabled annually to put on record the names of those, who have been ransomed from the grave. Within the last five years you number *one hundred and thirty-eight* persons, whom you have contributed to restore from the borders of destruction to the joys of life and the labours of society. This acknowledgment includes not the multitude of shipwrecked mariners on our coast, the merit of whose deliverance, in the same space of time, you do not exclusively claim, but in which the world allows you an honourable share.

Prosecute, multiply, and, if possible, improve your benevolent exertions for the preservation of seamen, whose useful lives are so intimately connected with labour and perils. Let their huts be continued, and, in some instances, better accommodated, for their reception, when, saved from the horrours of the sea, they are ready to perish on the shore. Already you have their thanksgivings and supplications to heaven on your behalf. But if their honest hearts are thankful for these proofs of your concern for their comfort, what will be their grat-

---

14 In the appendix to the Bishop of Gloucester's sermon preached before the Royal Humane Society in 1803, it is asserted, that, since the period of its institution, which was in 1774, the Society has been the means of preserving and restoring the lives of no less than 2,798 persons, who would, in former times, have suffered premature death and interment, so as to have been forever lost to their families, their friends, and the community.

itude, when they shall shortly behold the *Greathead Life-Boat*,[15] which you are building with so much care and expense, as a new token of your mercy for their sorrows, and as the ark of their future safety in moments of tempest and shipwreck ?

Surely it is better to be thus employed in " preserving life and alleviating its miseries," than in spreading havock and wretchedness over the face of the globe. Who would not rather possess the character and the reflexions of a Howard, than the dispositions and fame of the most splendid conqueror ? Blush, O ye sanguinary tyrants and ravagers of the earth, to think, that whilst the humane physician is incessantly toiling for the prolongation of human life, you are equally busy in contriving its waste. He adds treatise to treatise to improve the healing art ; you do the same to multiply the intsruments of destruction, and to arm them with new powers. He weeps, that a few noxious animals should be sacrificed for the benefit of discovery ; whilst you, after deluging a world with blood, lament that you cannot repeat the experiment.

But the friends of humanity are richly consoled in the choice and pursuit of their labours from considering the infinite worth of the human soul. In the frame and faculties, in the exertions, attainments, and whole history of man, they perceive his high destination. They see foresight in his plans, and ingenuity in his toils. By patience he converts the rude forest into flourishing fields and

---

[15] A Life Boat, after the model invented by Mr. Greathead, of South Shields, England, is now in forwardness, under the direction of Mr. E. Sigourney, and before the next anniversary will be fit for use. Of this invention see a copious account in the Amer. Ed. of Dr. Rees' New Cyclop. vol. v. part 1. art. *Life Boat*.

fruitful gardens, and barren shores into magnificent cities. With an enterprizing hand he ploughs the ocean, and, in imitation of Omniscience, ' numbers the stars of heaven, calling them all by their names.'[16] They behold him, in brief, made in the image of God, a ' little lower than the angels, crowned with glory and honour,'[17] and capable, through the culture of his intellectual and moral powers, of endless progression in knowledge, virtue, and felicity.

Yet is it a fact, that this being, so noble in form and godlike in faculties, is every moment obnoxious to an host of dangers, and to the evil of death in a multiplicity of forms. Moralists and poets have represented his life by similitudes, which, of all objects in nature, are distinguished for their frailty. ' It is grass,' say they, ' which in the morning groweth up, and in the evening is cut down and withered.'[18] ' It is a flower, which is crushed by the foot, blighted by the wind, nipped by the frost, felled by the worm. It is a shadow, a dream, a vapour, vanity, nothing. Such is the life of this lord of the lower creation. He, who can give a new path to the rivers of the wilderness, and disarm the clouds of their thunder ; he, who can bind nations together, separated by immeasurable oceans, is himself girded by the bands of death, and reluctantly[19] carried to the tomb. He, by whose voice a whole country is either blessed with peace, or cursed with war, and whose single nod gives law to an empire, ' hath no power over the spirit to retain the spirit in the day of death.'[20] By the instrumentality of a moth or a hair, ' his breath goeth forth, and in that very day his thoughts

[16] Ps. c. xlvii. 4.   [17] Heb. ii. 7.   [18] Ps. xc. 4.
[19] John xxi. 18.   [20] Eccl. viii. 8.

perish'.[21]   There is no ransom, which can alter his fate. His treasures, which the seas have submerged, may be redeemed from their miry bed, and the estates, of which fraud, or the fortune of war may have deprived him, may be restored and secured to his children ; but the principle of animation once extinct, it is beyond his utmost power,[22] and that of united creation, ' to cause breath to re-enter into his body, that he may live.'

What is the instruction, which is hence given to man ? He is taught the benefits of society.   Those arts, which evince the wonderful ingenuity and perseverance of the human mind, are the product not of savage, but of social life.   Alone, individuals of our race are weak ; united with their fellows, they are strong.   He, who in society can tame the fiercest beasts, construct impregnable castles, and direct the force of machines, almost sufficient to over-turn the solid globe, is in solitude helpless and inert ; un-able to repel the evils which assail him by means of muscular strength, and too indolent and timid for experi-ment.   It is in society, that he improves upon the designs and labours of his predecessors :   it is here, that he trans-forms the cottage into a palace, and the skin and the coarsest materials into silks :   it is here, that he substitutes the immense and beautiful ship, guided by a compass, for the frail bark, that durst not lose sight of the shore :   it is here, that, to form a register for his thoughts, he exchan-

---

21 Ps. cxlvi. 4.

22 Life is not to be bought with heaps of gold.
Not all Apollo's Pythian treasures hold
Can bribe the poor possession of a day :
Lost herds and treasures we by arms regain,
And steeds unrivalled on the dusty plain ;
But from our lips the vital spirit fled,
Returns no more to wake the silent dead

ges the cumbrous tablet for the convenient papyrus, and this for the accommodations and elegancies of the press : it is here, that medicine and physiology present their astonishing discoveries, in the room of senseless conceits and the tricks of astrologers ; it is, finally, here, that HUMANITY and RELIGION, the arts of doing good instead of evil, of saving and not destroying, place themselves on the ruins of cruelty and superstition, and assume the first rank among the arts of civilized life.[23]

We are also instructed from our subject to put a high value on human life. Without our knowledge or consent, the inspiration of the Almighty gave us existence,

[23] " Sweet is the voice that soothes my care,
 The voice of love, the voice of song ;
The lyre that celebrates the fair,
 And animates the warlike throng.

Sweet is the counsel of a friend,
 Whose bosom proves a pillow kind,
Whose mild persuasion brings an end
 To all the sorrows of the mind.

Sweet is the breath of balmy Spring,
 That lingers in the primrose vale ;
The wood-lark sweet, when on the wing,
 His wild notes swell the rising gale.

Sweet is the breeze, that curls the lakes,
 And early wafts the fragrant dew,
Through hovering clouds of vapour breaks,
 And clears the bright etherial blue.

Sweet is the walk, where daisies spring,
 And cowslips scent the verdant mead ;
The woodlands sweet where linnets sing,
 From every bold intruder freed.

BUT FAR MORE SWEET ARE VIRTUOUS DEEDS ;
 The hand that kindly brings relief,
The heart that with the widow's bleeds,
 And shares the drooping orphan's grief.

The PIOUS and HUMANE here rise
 With liberal hands and feeling heart :
And chase the tears from sorrow's eyes,
 And bid each noxious woe depart."

and, slender and precarious as our life is, we cannot end it without violence. Respiration, independently of care on our part, uninterruptedly proceeds, leaving us to sleep in security, to work with diligence, and. to study with composure. The inference hence is, that we are not our own. We are the creatures of God. He hath made us, and not we ourselves. Who art thou, then, rash mortal, that usurpest the prerogative of the Most High ? Who art thou, that presumest to destroy the life that was given thee ? Are you a soldier ? Stay, and complete your warfare. Have the courage to meet the dangers of your post, and await the dismissal of your commander. Are you a scholar ? Live, and finish your task. Learn the lessons, which are set you in the school of affliction and hardihood. Be ashamed and afraid of playing truant under the highest advantages and the most awful discipline. Think not, that the end of life is to eat, and to drink, and to play. You were made with far nobler views, than merely to feast and be feasted, to marry and be given in marriage, to preserve alive the name of an ancestor or the title of a family estate, to be misled by fools, or defrauded by knaves. You were made to be immortal. Of course you are placed in a mixed state, and were designed to breathe, not the pure oxygen air of sensitive delight, but the compound atmosphere of health and sickness, of labour and ease, of joy and sorrow. You are stationed in an apartment of the creator's works, not to be an idle and laughing spectator of the stupendous scenes around you, but to be interested, impressed, enlightened, and improved by all that you see, hear, and know. Yes, the culture of his intellectual and moral powers is the end of man's creation, and the means

through which he is designed to prolong his existence
under happier privileges. Of the ignorant and fool-
ish, the cruel and impious, we will now be silent ;
but the wise and good are destined to inherit a future and a blissful life. The hope of this happiness
we derive from the light of nature ; but its certainty
is the glorious intelligence of divine revelation. It
is the peculiar province of the gospel to assure us, that
God is both able by his power, and inclined by his good-
ness, to CAUSE BREATH TO ENTER INTO THE DEAD
BODIES OF THE HUMAN RACE, THAT THEY MAY
LIVE. This is a resuscitation infinitely more valuable,
than what the efforts of humanity can boast. We are
grateful to you, friends of science and lovers of mercy, for
restoring suspended respiration to those, whom the waves
had whelmed, or the mephitic gas had suffocated ; but
we are more thankful to the Son of God, who rescues the
nature of man from the dominion of eternal sleep, and
maintains an undisputed triumph over death and the grave.
Your intentions are merciful, but you cannot ensure to the
life you restore a happy issue. You sometimes recal the
subjects of your charity to a condition of hopeless wretchedness, often to the ills of poverty, and always to a scene
of temptation, disappointment, and toil. The most you
can give them is a short reprieve only from the power of
our common foe, who will eventually fold them in his icy
arms, scorning alike their entreaties and their resistance.
But the resurrection, of which Jesus Christ will make his
disciples the subjects, will introduce them to a life of
knowledge, unattended with the darkness and perplexities
of ignorance ; to a life of virtue, free from the arts of se-

duction ; to a life of liberty, without apprehensions of li-
centiousness ; to a life of glory, which cannot be tarnished
by disgrace ; to a life, in fine, which is encompassed by
no enemies, tormented by no fears, and can be ended by
no death.

Happy are they, who perform his commandments, that
the breath of immortality may enter into them, and that
they may live forever in that city of our God !

APPENDIX.

The following accounts of several shipwrecked mariners must appear interesting to the friends of humanity, and received the attention of the Society.

CAPT. Joel Phillibroke, and Capt. James Fuller, took on board their schooner, Capt. Thomas Chase, and his crew, consisting of twelve men, who were cast ashore at Boone bay, a desolate part of Newfoundland.

It appeared to the satisfaction of the Trustees, that the above named Phillabroke and Fuller were detained, in consequence of their humanity, a number of days at sea, by contrary winds, and were reduced to a short allowance for provisions ; and that Chase, with his people, would have suffered extremely through the winter, and probably most of them perished ; these fishing vessels being the last that were leaving the straits of Belleisle for the season. —Hence the premium of sixty dollars was voted, from a desire to encourage such acts of kindness, and every attention to poor ship-wrecked seamen.

> " When furious tempests raise the dashing wave,
> All ye who harbour safely on the land,
> Remember those who now the tempest brave,
> And lend, oh lend the friendly helping hand."

Another instance of preservation was in our own bay, within two leagues of the light-house.

CAPT. Thomas Knox, one of the members of the Society, was sitting at his window at the light-house, and saw a schooner overset. She was completely on her side. He called to one of his men, and ordered the boat out immediately ; but this man seeing a boat already under sail, beating up to Boston, the wind being very brisk at N. W. called to him, pointing to the vessel in distress. The boat belonged to Mr. Morgan, in which were several males and females. Morgan shifted his course, went down immediately to the schooner, and found several men holding to the keel, who,in a very few minutes, must have sunk in the water. It was peculiarly fortunate that Morgan's boat was in readiness, and that the wind favoured ; nothing else could have saved the lives of the people aboard the schooner, who were in such imminent danger. The schooner's name was Osborn, and belonged to Plymouth. The persons saved were Robert Finney, Caleb Churchill, Zaccheus Holmes, Samuel Allen, Samuel Morton, and William Evenor.

———•+•———

Medfield, 20 *Oct.* 1806.

DEAR SIR,

THROUGH you, I wish to communicate to the Trustees of our Humane Society, a statement of a successful exertion in saving the life of a lad, who had nearly perished in the watery element. I am satisfied, the activity and enterprise of the agents will be thought deserving of your attention.

Lowel Mason, a son of my nearest neighbour, of about 16, went into Charles river to bathe, and, unexpectedly to himself, was carried by the current where the water was 8 or 9 feet in depth. Having sunk, and arisen twice, calling for help, in the best manner his situation admitted, he went down the *third* time. Two lads, younger than himself, being present, viz. Moses Wight and Joseph Lovel, the former, with all his clothing upon him, plunged into the water, and brought his friend from the bottom ; while the other, very judiciously, floated a rail on the surface, and aided them both to the land.

Young Mason assures me, that from the time of his calling for help, he recollects nothing, until he found himself, supported at the shore by the hand of his friend.

The lads testify, that he appeared insensible, and was unable to support himself for some time ; that he emitted a considerable quantity of water, and gradually regained his recollection, and the use of his limbs, in such measure as to ride home, about $1\frac{1}{2}$ miles, in a waggon, with which he had been out on business for his parents. This is the testimony of the lads, which is all the nature of the case admits ; and I beg leave to add, their character leaves no room for doubt of its correctness.

With regards to the gentlemen united with you in the trust of the Society,   I am, dear sir,

Your friend and humble servant,

James Scott, Esq.   THO's PRENTISS.

To the Trustees of the Massachusetts Humane Society.

GENTLEMEN,

HAVING been favoured with the enclosed letter from Capt. Sylvanus Thomas, of Kingston, and viewing him as a man of honour and integrity, I communicate it to the Trustees for their consideration.   I am, with great respect,

Your most obed't humble serv't,

JAMES THACHER.

Kingston, June 16th, 1807.

Dr. JAMES THACHER.

DEAR SIR,

KNOWING that the objects of the institution of the Humane Society, of which you are a member, extend to almost every act of humanity, especially when the act appears to proceed from disinterested benevolence ; entertaining a profound respect for the excellent institution and its administration, I consider it my indispensable duty, (and I do it with deference) to communicate the following facts, through you, to the Society.

Travelling into the District of Maine, in March last, in company with Mr. Leonard Jarvis, just at night on the 21st, we accidentally fell in company with two young men, who were travelling

D

over the ferry at Lewistown, on the Androscoggin river ; arriving at the river, I requested one of the young men to lead my horse over on the ice, (which was represented safe) he accordingly led him on the ice about thirty feet, and the horse being thirsty, stopped to drink, (there being a little water on the ice.) I passed on the ice by them on to the river ; Jarvis led his horse on abreast of mine, and stopped also. Before I had got four rods from them, I perceived Jarvis' horse had broken through ; I instantly returned, and before I reached my horse, he slumped through also ; attempting to save him, the ice gave away from under me, and let me instantly into the water. Jarvis instantly followed. Thus were we, and both our horses, at once let into a swift current of water, ten feet deep, and only eight feet of the ice broken one way, and six the other. I called for help, which probably drew the young man's attention to me first. He stepped to the upper edge of the ice, and reached his hand to me, but the current was so strong, and swept me away so fast, that he could not reach me ; he returned, caught me, just as I struck the lower edge of the ice, and rescued me. He then cried, " for God's sake let's save this man," (Jarvis.) He caught him by the hand, who was then keeping himself from sinking by his horse's neck. I caught hold with him, and saved him. But his intrepidity did not end here—He appeared equally solicitous to save Mr. Jarvis' horse, (my horse having gone under) and by his activity and contrivance, we succeeded. Mr. Jarvis had been under several times, and was unable to stand when first taken out, but recovered without any extraneous aid.—I would observe, that the other young man never assisted us at all.

The young man who rescued us, has written me, (by my request) that his name is Grindal Caffin, of Unity, county of Kennebeck.

Being myself unable to bestow that pecuniary reward which such conduct merits, I have made this statement to the Society, which can, I presume, be substantiated by Mr. Jarvis, if necessary.

I am, your most ob't, and very humble serv't,

SYLVANUS THOMAS.

LIFE BOAT.

IT has been one of the objects of the Humane Society to pro-
vide a life boat,.which may prove the means of preserving many
mariners coming upon our coasts in the season of storms. There
is one now building at Nantucket, which will be finished in a
few weeks, and exhibited in the harbour of Boston. It is not yet
determined what part of the coasts is best to keep the boat the
ensuing season, but generally thought it will be somewhere near
the shores of Plymouth.

The inventor of the life boat is Henry Greathead, esq.* of
South Shields, England. For several years the ingenuity and labour of Mr. Greathead was not sufficiently remunerated. For
waving the idea of exclusive profit, when the preservation of life
was the object, he neglected to secure the patent, and even fur-
nished plans and models, from which the life boat might be con-
structed by others. The attention of the legislature was at length
attracted by the celebrity and usefulness of the scheme, and on
the report of a committee 1200*l.* was voted him by the house of
commons as a reward. He also received 100 guineas from several societies. And 2000 guineas were raised for encouraging
the building of life boats in several parts of Great Britain. An
elegant diamond ring was also sent him by the emperor of Russia.

The object of this useful invention is to save the lives of people wrecked on coasts. A plan and description of this boat were
taken from Mr. G.'s original by Col. Tatham, and sent by that
gentleman to Mr. Jefferson, president of the United States.

CONSTRUCTION.

THE boat to be built from a given length. The breadth is one
third of the length, with both ends alike. The keel of the boat is a
plank, bearing a proportional breadth in the mid-ships, narrowing
towards the ends to the thickness of the bottom of the stems, and
forming a convex downwards. The stems are the segment of a

* Vide Annual Report of London Humane Society, and Willich's Ency-
clopedia.

circle, with a considerable rake. The bottom section to the floor heads, is a curve with the sweep of the keel ; the floor head curving. A bilge plank is worked on each side, next the floor head, with a double rabbit groove, of a thickness nearly similar to the keel, on the outside of which are fixed two bilge trees corresponding nearly on a level with the keel. The ends of the bottom section form the part of the cable bow, more eliptical to the top, projecting considerably, each end the same. The sides from the floor heads to the top of the gunwale, flaunch on each side in proportion to nearly half the breadth.....The breadth of the boat is continued well towards the ends, leaving a sufficient length of straight side at the top. The shear is regular along the straight side, and more elevated towards the ends. The gunwale is fixed on the outside ; the outside is cased with cork the whole length of the regular shear, from the under part of the gunwale to twenty-three inches down the depth of the side. The cork has several thicknesses, so as to project at top a little without the gunwale, and is secured with plates of copper. The quantity of cork employed in the construction is about 700 wt. The thwarts are five in number, all stauntioned, and row double-banked, with ten oars. The oars are short, fixed by iron thole pins, and slung with graummets, to enable the rowers to pull either way. The boat is steered by an oar at either end, and the steering oar is one-third longer than the rowing oar. The platform, in the bottom, is placed horizontally. The length of the mid-ships, and the sides from the bottom to the under part of the thwarts, is cased with cork. At the ends, the platforms are more elevated, for the convenience of the steersman, and to give him a greater command of power with the oars.

PRACTICAL REMARKS.

" The curving keel and bottom permit the boat to be turned with facility ; she is kept more easily in equilibrium than any other shape ; is more easily steered, and safer among the breakers ; the great rake of the stems, and fine entrance below, forming part of the cable bow. ·This construction is superior to all others in a high sea and broken water ; and with the projection to the top of the gunwale, is the means, when the boat is conducted to head the sea, of dividing the waves which generally break into a common boat. The breadth being continued well to the ends, supports the boat when rowing against the waves ; and both ends being similar, she is always in a position to be rowed either way without turning. The addition of the staunchions under the thwarts, admit the boat-man to act with a firmer force, and in the instance of the boat's stri-ing the ground, the weight of the men, by the communication of the staunchions, will, in some degree, resist the shock. The ad-vantage of a short oar, in a high sea, is obvious. It is more man-ageable, and permits the rower to keep his seat ; but the long oar, in the midst of agitated waves, would be unwieldy, and the stroke frequently uncertain. The cork on the outside is a most excellent defence, and displaces a large column of water : and it has been proved by experience, to float the boat with the principal part of her bottom stove and loose. The great projection of the cork also, on the outside, prevents her being overturned. The best method of conducting the boat, is to head the sea ; which, from her con-struction, aided by the force of the oars, will launch her over the water with rapidity, without taking in any water.

" The person who steers the boat should be well acquainted with the course of the tides, in order to take every possible advan-tage ; and great care should be taken in approaching the wreck, that the boat be not damaged, as there is frequently a strong reflux of the sea near the wreck ; when the wind blows to the land, the boat will return to the shore before the wind and sea, without any other effort than steering. Signed

HENRY GREATHEAD."

Mr. GREATHEAD stated, " That he conceived the principle of his invention from the following idea, which had frequently occur-red to him, viz. Take a spheroid, and divide it into quarters, each quarter is eliptical, and nearly resembles the half of a wooden bowl, having a curvature with projecting ends ; this thrown into the sea, or broken water, cannot be upset, or lie with the bottom upwards."

The tesimony laid befor the committee of the House of Com-mons, by persons of credit who had either used the boat, or had witnessed its use by others, leaves no room to doubt of its being fully adequate to the purposes for which it was intended. ' Capt. GIL-FRED LOWSON REED, an elder brother of the Trinity-house, observed to the committee, " That when the sea does not tumble in upon the beach very much, the boat may be easily launched by laying the ways as far as possible in the water, and the carriage hauled from under her : when there is a great sea on the beach, the boat must be launched from the carriage before she comes to the surf, on planks laid across, as other boats are launched, the people standing on the ends to prevent the sea moving them ; then, with the assistance of the anchor and cable (which has been laid out at sea for that purpose) the boat's crew would draw her over the highest sea.

" Upon the boat returning to the shore, two double blocks are provided, and having a short strop fixed in the hole, in the end of the boat next the sea, the boat is easily drawn upon the carriage."

———

In the last publication of the Humane Society, mention is made of the appointment of a committee to take into consideration the application of a number of gentlemen in the town of Duxborough, for one or more huts to be erected on their beach, near the Gurnet, where several vessels have been wrecked, and whole crews lost ; some of whom perished on the shore for want of places of shelter. The committee visited the spot in the month of October, and with the advice of those who were well acquainted with the ground, fixed upon two spots, where huts were erected, and supplied with every necessary for such as might be wrecked. The situation is as follows. Duxborough beach, formerly called Salt's beach, is about seven miles long, running from the Gurnet light house to the Southmost point. The distance from the Plymouth light house to the Southmost hut is two miles and a half, and about half a mile from the high pines. The other hut is erected two miles and a half north of the hut abovementioned, which is about half a mile south of Rouse's Hammock.

Premiums adjudged and paid from June 1806, *to June* 1807.

George Brown, for taking up a child that fell off a wharf . .	$ 1 50
John Wheeler do.	2
James Marshal and John Carlin 3 dolls. each, for taking up several persons overset in a boat between Boston and Noddle's island	6
David Nelson, for taking a child out of the Dock	1
Richard Thayer for saving a boy's life	3
Benjamin Tarbox for his signal exertions in saving a child from drowning, that fell into a well ninety feet deep, at Castle William	10
Samuel Polley, for taking up a person near drowning . .	3
Moses Wight $5, and Joseph Lovel $2, for saving a lad from drowning	7
Samuel Morgan, for saving several persons from drowning in Boston bay	5
James Fuller and Joel Phillibroke, $30 each, for saving capt. Thomas Chase, with twelve other persons, from the wreck of the schooner, called the Welcome Return of Bath, who were in imminent danger of perishing on a desolate coast	60
Willard Richardson, for his signal exertions in saving the life of a man	10

$ 108 50

Expenses of the Society.

Semiannual meeting	11
Parker's account for Mr. Harris's Sermon	70
Huts on Duxborough beach, including several accounts . . .	163 54
Capt. Scott's bill of expenses for hut on Lovel's island, &c.	30 26
Thomas Smalley's account, moving a hut, &c.	11 21
Paid Mr. Burge, messenger of the society	36

Total $ 430 51

Property of the Society.

Certificates, six per cents.	1529 46 }	
Deferred do.	378 22 } real value	1329 27
Eight per cents.		800
Three per cents.		791 25
Massachusetts state note		3068 64
Union Bank stock		2035 17
West Boston bridge		417 17
Malden bridge fund		694 58

$ 9136 08

OFFICERS OF THE SOCIETY.

MEMBERS DECEASED SINCE THE LAST PUBLICATION.

CATALOGUE OF THE MEMBERS OF THE SOCIETY.

Names and Places of Abode.

A

His Excellency John Adams, *late President of the United States.*
Mr. Philip Adams,
Samuel Abbot,
Judah Alden, *Duxbury,*
Jeremiah Allen, Esq.
Mr. William Allen,
Rev. Mr. Thomas Allen, *Pittsfield.*
Mr. Thomas Amory,
Mr. Thomas C. Amory,
Mr. Jonathan Amory, jun.
John Andrews, Esq.
Mr. James Andrews,
Mr. John Trecothick Apthorp,
Mr. Nathan Appleton,

Mr. Charles Atkinson,
Capt. Henry Atkins,
Capt. Silas Atkins,
Jonathan L. Austin, Esq.
Richard Austin.

B

Adam Babcock, Esq.
Nathaniel Balch, Esq.
Mr. George Bailies,
Loammi Baldwin, Esq. *Woburn.*
Luke Baldwin, Esq.
Rev. Thomas Baldwin, D.D.
Mr. John Ballard,
Mr. Christopher Barker,
Rev. Thomas Barnard, D. D. *Salem.*
Capt. Tristram Barnard,
Mr. John Barrett, *Quincy.*
Dr. Josiah Bartlett, *Charlestown.*
Mr. George Bartlett, *do.*
Dr. Thomas Bartlett,
Mr. Joseph Bartlett, *Plymouth.*
Dr. Zacheus Bartlett, *do.*
James Bird,
Jeremiah Belknap,
Mr. Samuel Blagge,
Mr. Asahel Bigelow,
Mr. Edward Blake,
Mr. George Blanchard,
Samuel Blodget, Esq. *Haverhill.*
Mr. William Boardman, jun.
Jeremiah S. Boies, *Milton.*
Mr. Kirk Boot,
John B. Bowen,
Hon. James Bowdoin, Esq.
John Boyle, Esq.
Mr. John Boyle, jun.
Ward Nicholas Boylston, Esq. *Roxbury.*
Mr. Charles Bradbury,
Capt. Gamaliel Bradford,
Mr. Dudley A. Bradstreet,
Major John Bray,
Samuel Breck, Esq. *Philadelphia.* 33 : 33
Mr. Eben. Breed, *Charlestown.*

E

Mr. William Breed,
Mr. Thomas Brewer,
Mr. John Brewer, *No. 4, Passamaquoddy.*
Mr. Oliver Brewster,
Hon. E. Bridge, Esq. *Chelmsford.*
Mr. Matthew Bridge, *Charlestown.*
Mr. Nathan Bridge, *do.*
Mr. Andrew Brimmer,
George W. Brimmer,
Henry Broomfield, Esq. *Harvard.*
Mr. William Brown,
Rev. Joseph S. Buckminster,
Charles Bulfinch, Esq.
Mrs. Caroline Bullard, *Medfield.*
Mr. Jeremiah Bumstead, jun.
Mr. Josiah Bumstead,
Mr. George Burroughs, jun.
Rev. Jonathan Burr, *Sandwich.*
Capt. William Burrows,
Benjamin Bussey, Esq.
Hon. Peter C. Brooks, Esq.
Mr. Thomas Burley.

C

Honourable George Cabot, Esq.
Mr. Samuel Cabot,
Mr. William Cabot, *Concord.*
Mr. Joseph Callender, jun.
Mr. Benjamin Callender,
Samuel Carey, Esq. *Chelsea.*
Mr. James Carter,
Mr. Edward Cazneau,
Mr. Gardner L. Chandler,
Capt. Jonathan Chapman,
Mr. Joseph Chapman,
Mr. Henry Chapman,
Peter Chase, *Nantucket.*
Asaph Churchill,
Rev. John Cheverus,
Mr. Benjamin Coates,
Mr. Richard Clabby,
Francis D. Channing, Esq.
Rev. William Channing,
Mr. John Chipman, *Sandwich.*

Benjamin Clark, Esq.
Mr. William Cleland,
J. Smith Colburn,
Mr. Joseph Coolidge,
Cornelius Coolidge,
Samuel Cooper, Esq.
Thomas Coffin,
J. G. Coffin,
Mr. Samuel Coverly,
Mr. Elisha Crocker,
Mr. Allen Crocker,
Mr. Andrew Cunningham,
John Cunningham,
Joseph L. Cunningham,
Capt. Nathaniel Curtis,
Mr. Thomas Curtis,
Hon. William Cushing, Esq. *Scituate.*
Hon. Nathan Cushing, Esq. *Scituate.*
Rev. John Cushing, *Ashburnham.*
Thomas Cushing,
Charles Cushing, Esq.
Benjamin Clark Cutler, Esq. *Roxbury.*
Mr. James Cutler,
Samuel Clap, Esq.
Nathan Clarke,
Capt. Edward Cruft.

D

Hon. Francis Dana, Esq. *Cambridge.* $3 : 33
Hon. Samuel Dana, Esq. *Groton.*
Mr. Benjamin Dana,
Dexter Dana.
Mr. John Dabney, *Salem.*
Mr. William Dall,
Peter Roe Dalton, Esq.
Dr. Thomas Danforth,
Mr. Isaac Davenport,
Amasa Davis, Esq.
Hon. John Davis, Esq.
Mr. Isaac P. Davis,
Mr. Samuel Davis, *Plymouth.*
Mr. William Davis, *do.*
Joshua Davis, Esq.

Aaron Davis, *Roxbury.*
Joseph Davis, *do.*
Mr. Jonathan Davis,
Hon. Thomas Dawes, Esq.
Hon. Thomas Dawes, jun. Esq.
William Dehone,
Thomas Dennie, Esq.
Hon. Elias H. Derby, Esq. *Salem.*
Richard Devens, Esq. *Charlestown.*
Hon. Samuel Dexter, Esq. *Mendon.* $2 : 25
Aaron Dexter, M.D.
Andrew Dexter, jun. Esq.
Benjamin Delano,
Capt. Thomas Dean,
Mr. Isaac Dupee,
Mr. Thomas Dickason, *London.*
Rev. Timothy Dickenson, *Holliston.*
Mr. Samuel B. Doane,
Mr. Samuel A. Dorr,
Mr. Ebenezer Dorr,
Samuel Dunn, Esq.
Alpheus Dunham,
John Derby, Esq.
Gamaliel L. Dwight,
Andrew Dunlap.

E

Rev. Joseph Eckley, D.D.
Samuel Eliot, Esq.
Rev. John Eliot,
Justin Ely, Esq. *West-Springfield.*
Rev. William Emerson.

F

Mr. James Farrar,
Mr. Ebenezer Farley,
Mr. Richard Faxon,
John Fenno,
John Fleet, M.D.
Jeremiah P. Fogg,
Mr. Thomas Fleet,
Hon. Dwight Foster, Esq. *Brookfield.*
Mr. James H. Foster,

Henry Fowle,
Hon. Samuel Fowler, Esq. *West-field.*
Mr. Samuel A. Frazier, *Dux-boro'.*
Mr. Ebenezer Francis,
Rev. James Freeman,
Dr. Nathaniel Freeman, *Sand-wich.*
Mr. James Freeman,
Benjamin Fuller.

G

Mr. Abraham W. Gammage,
Mr. Caleb Gannett, *Cambridge.*
Rev. John Sylvester John Gardiner,
John Gardner, Esq.
Eben Gay, Esq. *Hingham.*
Hon. Elbridge Gerry, Esq. *Cambridge.*
J. T. Gilman,
Thacher Goddard,
Mr. Benjamin Goddard,
Mrs. Goddard,
Nathaniel Goodwin, Esq. *Plymouth.*
Simeon Goodwin,
Capt. Nathaniel Goodwin,
Capt. Ozias Goodwin,
Randolph Goodwin, *Dresden.*
Mr. Samuel Gore,
Stephen Gorham, Esq.
Mr. Moses Grant,
Mr. Moses Grant, jun.
Mr. Benjamin Gray,
Mr. William R. Gray,
Mr. Sylvanus Gray,
Edward Gray, Esq.
Francis Greene, Esq. *Medford.*
Mr. Gardner Greene,
John R. Greene,
James Greene, *Charlestown.*
Joseph Greenleaf, Esq.
Daniel Greenleaf, *Quincy.*
Oliver C. Greenleaf,
David S. Greenough, Esq. *Roxbury.*

Rev. William Greenough, *Newton.*
Richard Green.

H

Mr. Nathaniel Hall, *Chelsea.*
Joseph Hall, Esq.
Samuel Hammond,
William Hammatt, Esq.
Charles Hammatt,
Benjamin Hammatt,
Ebenezer Hancock, Esq.
Mr. Thomas Hancock,
Mr. John Hancock,
Mr. Moses Bullen Harden, *Medfield.*
Edward Harris,
Rev. Thaddeus M. Harris, *Dorchester.*
Mr. Jonathan Harris,
Oliver Hartshorn,
Mr. James Harrison, *Charlestown.*
Elisha Hathaway,
Mr. Judah Hays,
Mr. Ralph Haskins,
Dr. Lemuel Hayward,
Dr. Nathan Hayward, *Plymouth.*
Caleb Hayward,
John Heard, jun. Esq.
Joseph Head,
Mr. Barnabas Hedge, *Plymouth,*
Hon. Samuel Henshaw, Esq. *Northampton.*
Hon. Stephen Higginson, Esq.
Stephen Higginson, jun. Esq.
Mr. George Higginson,
Henry Hill, Esq.
Mr. David Hinckley,
Hon. Benjamin Hitchborn, Esq.
John Holland,
Hon. Samuel Holden, Esq. *Danvers.*
Henry Homes   &2
Maj. Samuel Howard, *Augusta.*
Dr. John Clark Howard,
Mr. Joseph Howe,
Jonathan Hunnewell, Esq.

Hon. E. Hunt, Esq. *Northampton.*
Mr. Samuel Hunt,
Mr. Augustus Hunt,
Mr. Enoch Huse,
Capt. Henry Hubbart,
Nr. Henry Hunter,
Mr. Joseph Hurd, *Charlestown.*
Dr. Isaac Hurd, *Concord.*
Mr. Zacheus Hussey, *Nantucket.*
William V. Hutchins.

I

Mr. Daniel Ingalls.

J

Hon. Jonathan Jackson, Esq.
Henry Jackson, Esq.
Mr. John Jackson, *Charlestown.*
Edward Jackson, Esq.
Patrick Jeffrey, Esq. $10. *Milton.*
Mr. John Jenks, *Salem.*
Mr. Joseph W. Jenkins,
Hon. John Coffin Jones, Esq.
Stephen Jones, jun.
Mr. Thomas K. Jones.
Dr. John Joy,
Mr. Benjamin Joy,
Mr. William Jackson,
Mr. William Jepson.

K

Rev. John T. Kirkland, D.D.
Mr. Josiah Knapp,
Mrs. Susanna Kneeland,
Mr. Jacob Kuhn,
Mr. John Kuhn,
Mr. William Kempton,
Rev. James Kendall, *Plymouth.*
Mr. John King,
Oliver Keating.

L

Mr. Robert Lamb,
Mr. William Lambert, *Roxbury.*
Mr. Joseph Larkin,
Rev. John Lathrop, D.D.
Mr. Samuel C. Lathrop,
Mr. Caleb Leach, *Plymouth.*

Mr. Ebenezer Lewis,
Hon. Benja. Lincoln, *Hingham.*
John I. Linzee,
James Lloyd, M.D.
James Lloyd, jun. Esq.
Mr. Caleb Loring,
John Lowell, Esq.
Rev. Mr. Charles Lowell,
Isaac Lathrop, Esq. *Plymouth.*
Mr. Joseph Lovering,
John Lucas, Esq. *Brookline.*

M

Capt. Mungo Mackay,
Capt. James M'Gee,
Rev. Joseph M'Kean,
Mr. Edward M'Lane,
Mr. John M'Lean,
Mr. John Marston,
Mr. Simeon Mason,
Hon. Jonathan Mason, Esq.
Hon. Ebenezer Mattoon, *Amherst.*
Mr. John Maynard,
Col. John May,
Col. Joseph May,
Mr. Samuel May,
Mr. John May, jun.
Rev. John Mellen, *Cambridge.*
Mr. Nathaniel Merriam,
William Minot, Esq.
Capt. Daniel Messenger,
Mr. James Morril,
Rev. Jedidiah Morse, D.D. *Charlestown.*
Rev. John Murray,
Thomas Melville, Esq.
Allen Melville,
Jonathan Merry.

N

Mr. Joseph Newel,
Mr. John Nicholson, *Medfield.*
Mr. Perkins Nichols,
George Noble.

O

Ebenezer Oliver,

Dr. Cushing Otis, *Scituate.*
Mr. John Osborne,
Mr. Francis J. Oliver,
Capt. James Odell.

P

Hon. Robert T. Paine, Esq.
Mr. William Paine,
Hon. Nathaniel Paine, Esq. *Worcester.*
Capt. Nehemiah Parsons,
Mr. Gorham Parsons,
Mr. John Parker,
Samuel Parkman, Esq.
Eliphalet Pearson, L.L.D. *Cambridge.*
Mr. John Peck, *Newton.*
Mr. Ebenezer Pemberton, *Billerica.*
Hon. Thomas H. Perkins, Esq.
Thomas Perkins, Esq.
Charles Phelps, Esq. *Hadley.*
Charles P. Phelps,
William Phillips, Esq.
James Phillips,
Hon. John Phillips, Esq. *Andover.*
Mr. Isaac Pierce,
Mr. Joseph Pierce,
John Pitts, Esq.
Rev. John Pipon, *Taunton.*
Mr. Nahum Piper,
Mr. Joseph Pope,
Mr. William Pratt,
Mr. Ebenezer Preble,
Rev. Thomas Prentiss, *Medfield.*
James Prentiss,
Mr. Samuel J. Prescott,
James Prince, Esq.
Edward Proctor, Esq.

Q

Hon. Josiah Quincy, Esq.

R

Joseph W. Revere,
Col. Paul Revere,
Mr. Benjamin Rich,

Chandler Robbins, Esq. *Hallowell.*
Col. James Robinson,
Mr. Henry N. Rogers,
Mr. John M. Russell,
Maj. Benjamin Russell,
Mr. John Richardson,
Mr. Eben Rollins,
Capt. Thomas Rogers.

S

His Excellency James Sullivan, Esq.
Hon. Caleb Strong, Esq.
Mr. Charles Savage,
William Savage,
Mr. Francis Sales,
Mr. Samuel Sanger,
Mr. Samuel Salisbury,
Mr. Samuel Salisbury, jun,
Daniel Sargeant, Esq.
Samuel G. Sargeant, *Charlestown.*
Eppes Sargeant,
Ignatius Sargeant,
David Sawyer,
William Scollay, Esq.
James Scott, Esq.
Doct. Charles L. Segars, *Northampton.*
Hon. William Seaver, Esq. *Kingston.*
Hon. David Sewall, Esq. *York.*
Hon. Samuel Sewall, Esq. *Marblehead.*
William N. Shaw,
Doct. William Sheldon, *Springfield.*
Hon. William Sheppard, Esq. *Westfield.*
H. Sheafe,
Mr. Elisha Sigourney,
H. Sigourney,
Andrew Sigourney,
William Smith, Esq.
Abiel Smith, Esq.
Dr. Nathaniel Smith,
Capt. George G. Smith, *Danvers.*

Mr. B. Smith,
Mr. Barney Smith,
Mr. Samuel Smith,
Mr. Samuel Snelling,
William Spooner, M.D.
Capt. Edward Staples,
William Stackpole,
William Stephenson, Esq.
Gideon Snow,
Mrs. Esther Sprague, *Dedham.*
Mr. Zebina Stebbins, *Springfield.*
Hon. William Stedman, Esq. *Lancaster.*
Ebenr. Storer, Esq. (deceased.)
Mr. Bradstreet Story,
Thomas W. Storrow,
Juan Stoughton, Esq. *Spanish Consul.*
Mr. Russell Sturgis,
Mr. Nathan Sturgis,
William Sullivan, Esq.
Mr. John L. Sullivan,
Thomas Sumner,
Mr. George Sutherland,
Mr. Samuel Swett.

T

Mr. Thomas Tarbell,
Rev. Thomas Thacher, *Dedham.*
Doct. James Thacher, *Plymouth.*
Doct. Thomas Thaxter, *Hingham.*
Mr. Obadiah Thayer,
Dr. Stephen Thayer,
Nathaniel Thayer,
Mr. Samuel M. Thayer,
Minot Thayer, *Braintree.*
Hon. Joshua Thomas, Esq. *Plymouth.*
Dr. Joshua Thomas,
William Thurston, Esq.
Mr. James Thwing,
David Tilden,
Joseph Tilden,
B. P. Tilden,
Mr. Jacob Tidd,
Mr. John Tileston,

Samuel Todd,
Mr. Abraham Touro,
Mr. Isaac Townsend,
Mr. Samuel Topliffe,
Mr. Samuel Torrey,
Capt. Eben. Torry, *Lancaster.*
John Tucker, Esq.
Richard D. Tucker,
Mr. Edward Tuckerman,
Mr. Edward Tuckerman, jun.
Rev. Joseph Tuckerman, *Chelsea.*
William Tuckerman,
G. Washington Tuckerman,
Hon. William Tudor, Esq.
Hon. Dudley A. Tyng, Esq.
Mr. Turell Tuttle.

W

Mr. Henry Wainwright,
Rev. B. Wadsworth, *Danvers.*
Ebenr. Wales, Esq. *Dorchester.*
Thomas B. Wales,
Capt. William Wall,
Mr. Lynde Walter,
Mr. Joseph Wiggin,
Mr. George Wheeler,
Mr. Moses Wheeler,
John Welles,
Thomas Wigglesworth,
John H. Wheelwright,
Abiel Wood, jun. *Wiscasset.*
Samuel Wheelwright,
Samuel H. Walley, Esq. $10.
Mr. William Walter,
Col. Joseph Ward, *Newton.*
Hon. A. Ward, Esq. *Charlestown.*
John Warren, M.D.
Henry Warren, Esq. *Plymouth.*
John C. Warren, M.D.
Mr. John Waters,
Thomas Welsh, jun.
Nathan Webb,
Capt. Thomas Webb,
David Webb,
Titus Welles,
Hon. Oliver Wendell, Esq.
Ezra Weston, *Duxboro'.*

Rev. Samuel West, D.D.
Mr. David West,
Mr. Jacob Weston,
Daniel Weston, Esq. *Eastport*.
Mr. James White,
Mr. Ebenezer Withington,
Jonathan Whitney,
Benjamin Whitman, Esq.
Mr. Davis Whitman,
Kilborn Whitman, Esq. *Pembroke*.
Mr. Ezra Whitney.
Mr. Samuel Whitwell,
Mr. William Whitwell,
Mr. William Williams,

E. Williams, Esq. *West-Stockbridge*.
Thomas Williams, jun. Esq. *Roxbury*.
Dr. Charles W. Winship, *Roxbury*.
John Winslow,
John Winslow, jun.
Dr. Isaac Winslow, *Marshfield*.
Thomas L. Winthrop, Esq.
Capt. John Foster Williams,
Mr. Eliphalet Williams,
Mr. Thomas Williams,
Henry H. Williams, *Roxbury*.

HONORARY MEMBERS.

Nathaniel Adams, Esq. *Portsmouth*.
Dr. Oliver Baron, *Calcutta*.
Rev. Andrew Brown, D.D. *Edinburg*.
Thomas Bulkley, Esq. *Lisbon*.
Ammi Ruhamah Cutter, M.D. *Portsmouth*.
Capt. John Calef, *St. Christophers* (West-Indies.)
Hon. Oliver Ellsworth, *late Chief Justice of the United States*.
Anthony Fothergill, M.D. *Bath*.
Edward Goodwin, M.D. *Bath*.
William Hawes, M.D. *London*.
Hon. Jedidiah Huntington, *New-London*.
John C. Lettsom, M.D. *London*.
Hon. David Ramsay, Esq. *Charleston, S. C.*

His Excellency John Langdon, Esq. *Portsmouth*.
Hon. Thomas Fraser, Esq. *London*.
Dr. John Osborne, *Middletown*, (Connecticut.)
Hon. Timothy Pickering, Esq. *Salem*.
Dr. Benjamin Rush, *Philadelphia*.
William Russell, Esq. *Middletown*, (Connecticut.)
Right Hon. Earl of Stamford, *London*.
Hon. James Sheafe, Esq. *Portsmouth*.
Hon. Samuel Tenny, Esq. *Exeter*.
Rev. Timothy Alden, *Portsmouth*.
Hon. Nicholas Gilman, *Exeter*.

Two hundred and one of the above have been admitted since the first day of June last.

Lightning Source UK Ltd.
Milton Keynes UK
UKHW011149051118
331792UK00005B/255/P